MW00583346

STARFALL

IN THE TEMPLE

A BOOK OF POEMS

with joy!

Prartho Sereno

BLUE LIGHT PRESS
1st WORLD
PUBLISHING

San Francisco | Fairfield | Delhi

Starfall in the Temple

Copyright ©2023 by Prartho Sereno

First Edition.

ISBN: 978-1-4218-3547-1

Library of Congress Cataloging-in-Publication Data

All rights reserved. Printed in the United States of America. No part of this book may be used or reproduced in any manner whatsoever without written permission except in the case of brief quotations embodied in critical articles and reviews.

Cover image from the mixed-media painting *Starfall in the Temple* (2022) by Prartho Sereno
Cover Design by Angelina Sereno

For information contact:

1ST WORLD LIBRARY
PO Box 2211
Fairfield, Iowa 52556
www.1stworldpublishing.com

BLUE LIGHT PRESS
www.bluelightpress.com
Email: bluelightpress@aol.com

Also by Prartho Sereno:

Poetry

Indian Rope Trick
Elephant Raga
Call from Paris
Causing a Stir: The Secret Lives & Loves of Kitchen Utensils
Garden Sutra (a chapbook)

Essays

Everyday Miracles: An A to Z Guide to the Simple Wonders of Life

Editor

Pandemic Puzzle Poems (co-edited with Diane Frank)
Everyday Osho: 365 Daily Meditations for the Here & Now

STARFALL

IN THE TEMPLE

A BOOK OF POEMS

꧁

This one's for the full caboodle:

my parents Grant & Geraldine,
siblings Gail, Gary, Ginene, Greg, & Gil.
For my sweetheart Dennis,
daughters: Drisana & Angelina,
and grandchildren: Quincy & Nautica,
Jazmine, Brandon, & Ziyah

… for the joyful chaos
you've brought & bring

꧁

In four billion years, our star will follow its fate, collapsing into a white dwarf. We exist only by chance, after all. The Voyager will still be sailing into the interstellar shorelessness on the wings of the "heavenly breezes" Kepler had once imagined, carrying Beethoven on a golden disc crafted by a symphonic civilization that long ago made love and war and mathematics on a distant blue dot.

~ Maria Popova

CONTENTS

III

TABLE OF CORRESPONDENCES

The underwater tug we call ebb tide
the seaweed knows as longing

The lilac we've deemed common
is known to the bee as Rapture of the Deep

These clouds we've named cumulus
the sky praises as bread

The ones we've come to know as raven
appear to the moon as flickers of grief

What we call wind in the tule grass
is known to the earth as the happiness
too delicate to name

l

so silent and unencumbered
over the waters

TEMPLE

He brought me there in our earliest days—
to the disarray of chiseled rock
behind the teahouse in Golden Gate Park.

It was where he found himself as a boy,
he said, deep in the spell of ruins.

They'd arrived by ship, the stones—
a disassembled monastery, crated,
marked, and mapped for reassembly.

But in the sacred way of things, the market
crashed and the boxed-up dream changed hands

and hands again until in a brilliant streak of grace
the crates went up in flames, markings erased, plans
gone to ash. And then the dispersal: Stones

rolled to the edge of the lake—prayer stools
among the cormorants and geese. Chunks
of the old cathedral hidden in plain sight—

beside the summer Ferris wheel for children
to stand tall in line or at the top of the wooded

trail in the kind gesture of a rock-mover
toward the weary. A generous haphazard
heap remained behind the teahouse

where barefoot boys imagined forts
for their pint-sized battles in their pint-sized
theaters of war. I'm sorry to say

on our last visit we were stunned to find most
of them gone. They'd been gathered up,
we were told, by a dedicated brotherhood—

the cathedral rebuilt, stones recloistered.
I'm sorry—sorry for the climbing boys and for

the cormorants and for you who look for rest
at the top of the trail. But I hope you'll go back
anyway. To walk the path or sit in the grass

by the lake. True, without the recomposed
arches and domes there'll be no heavenly echo
when your prayers are released, but they'll fly
so silent and unencumbered over the waters.

DIAGRAMMING THE SENTENCE

Our subject is *light*.
Modified by the stained glass window
and the silt-gray puddle beyond the porch
where sparrows come to bathe.

Our predicate is *searches*.
No modifier—there are no limits
to the longings of light.

Our object is understood,
meaning we have no words
for what light seeks,
but we can feel our way;
we know how light
likes to dance with the world—
co-conspirator, co-conjuror,
the original sweet whisperer
of nothings.

Ours, then, could be called
a simple sentence. Nothing
to compound our seeker,
who (unknown to her)
is a creature herself
of light. No relative
clauses. No infinitives
to split, no participle left
to dangle.

3

MIRRORED PALACE

If we're honest as we look in, Dear Reader, don't we
come upon a certain sorrow that is ours to carry—
a dark and sacred something we might call gravitas?
And if we allow ourselves a sidewise glance, don't we
sometimes catch a shy but insistent light that bends
(one might even say bows) to that dark seed?
Forgive me then as I wonder

which came first—Einstein's thoughts
about gravity warping space or the bearing witness
to his own sorrow as it bent the light. Which
came first—the quiet depths we humans
have always sensed around us or the matter
scientists have finally brought to light—
the incalculable darknesses that hold it all?

The human heart has its secret knowings;
the brain its fondness for fashion and fad.
There was a time when great thinkers saw fairies,
kept leather-bound ledgers with drawings and dates.

But the poles shifted and we were turned from
those iridescent ones toward functional gray,
were asked to refrain from the sidewise glance, to retrain
our visions to timepiece, engine, and grid. To pull
up our bootstraps and take to the tarmacs of reason.

We put on corrective lenses—what we once
called stars in their falling were recast as rogue
bits of dust and ice. *Real stars don't fall,* they
told us. *They're held by an absence so dense
there's no making heads or tails.*

But isn't the human brain—the one that construes
the paradigms and maps the stars—isn't it the very
one that circumnavigates the grocery, the very same
that falls in love, makes the coffee, does the math?

And whether we choose a turtle to ride us
through the firmament or prefer it all to pop
from a nanoscopic dot... Whatever
the unlikely tale, who can argue

that it's done with mirrors? For no matter
        how deep we dig, we come up
                facing ourselves.

VANISHING POINT

I ask the captain why we've dropped
anchor here on the open sea. What
does he see in the relentless collapse
of waves, in this splintering of light?
What does he hear between squawking gulls
and the heaving lull
of sirens' sobs against the hull?

He doesn't answer… his furrowed face
stained green by the sea.

From here there is no point
where lines converge for perspective.
No detail to vanish by degrees—
no street lamps or telephone poles
or wind-whittled cypress to dwindle away
single-file and disappear.

From here all things are close
and all of it unreachable.

Stars drop around us like snow,
sea-salt polishes the spyglass sky
to an impossibly lucid blue.

EVENT HORIZONS

A man now, my grandson has moved in downstairs
where he wrestles with the angels of amazement
and doubt. Our shadows bow to one another
as he leaves to drive people to the airport or city jobs.
I want to tell him things, but the guardians of predawn
won't let a whisper pass at this hour and I'm asleep

again before he comes home. I want to tell him
things, but the words have gotten snagged
in the brain's frayed cogs. The name,
for example, for the lightness
that can blow through a heart, lift it
from the body and sail it round the world.

I want to tell him, too, how the Unexpected
has a thing for us, how she hides among the pots
and pans, in wait for our little lives to whistle by.
And how nobody ever believes they are old.
One day you and your little-old-lady sweetheart
will make jokes about your slipping disguises
over scrambled eggs and toast.

NEGATIVE CAPABILITY

It's fire season in California and I'm on the downtown
library lawn thinking about 80-mile-an-hour winds.
I'm thinking about the traffic jam out of Paradise
and the artist who lost everything, but learned,
she said, to paint with her eyes.

Smoke surges into the valley; evacuation orders
in nearby towns. Here, whatever we do with power
has been cut off. We're a late October ghost town
with a line at the resuscitated phone booth—the mad dig
for quarters and the five-year-old with phone
to his ear, confused by his father's instructions,
asking, *What's a dial tone?*

I left home to stir and steep in the quiet. With our usual
frenzied buzz brought down to the register of falling
leaves and whir of hummingbird, I'd hoped
the tree-lined walk into town might be haunted
by silence. Which it is… with silence and light-
spattered shadows you can paint with your eyes.

THE BUTTERFLY EFFECT

When the unkempt girl whose eyes
are always fixed on something
the rest of us can't see leaps up
midway through the day's poem
to wildly swivel her arms,
does the breeze she becomes

touch the heads of the peonies,
bringing their tight buds
to unwind and let go
a perfumed eddy so dense

it draws in the disbelievers
and shipwrecked sailors
the unhappy housewives
and long-lost heralds of dawn

so that when the girl arrives home to drop
her heavy pack on the floor and search
the vacant lots of her mother's eyes

does she find at last a gardener
whistling in with his wheelbarrow
and trowel, come to shape the clouds
into polar bears and possums,
put in a patch of sweetgrass,
rows of wild peas?

PARTICLES & WAVES

Not one straight limb
in the bentwood rocker—
my favorite seat

         *   *   *

Beetle in that phosphorescent cloak
have you been visiting
the Northern Lights?

         *   *   *

Lemon tree's first year—one
sweet fruit with Saturday's fish
one more to go

         *   *   *

They beg me to come down
when I hover at the ceiling
    in dreams
    where I've remembered
    how to fly

         *   *   *

Teapot in the shape
of the Taj Mahal—
    threads of midnight
    spill into afternoon

          *   *   *

Nobody remembered
to take out the trash
till it fell on me—
this downpour of stars

          *   *   *

Houseful of trinkets:
potted plants, poetry books,
hand-turned bowls—
the bewildering magnet
of human want

          *   *   *

When I ask my grandson
how he plans to pay for the heap
of ephemera he's piled into my cart
    he's quick with the math:
    He has two wiggly teeth.

CHARLIE CHAPLIN & ME

Legend has it that Charlie Chaplin placed third
in a Charlie Chaplin Look-Alike Contest. Now
that I've been threatened suit for stealing a stranger's
pic for my publicity photo, I know how he feels.

When we met with an arbiter (it got that far),
she pointed to the leg in the photo and said, *Look
at the bulge of that calf—that's not your leg.*

Look at the flounce of those side-curls, she said.
That's not the way your hair goes—it's mine.

I'm embarrassed to admit how unsettling
it was. I found myself defensive, coming up
with details about the day my daughter snapped it:
On a walk by the lake, under an old madrone.

No, she said with a certainty I couldn't match.
*This was taken at the bus stop on College Ave—
See the shadow of oak leaves on my face?*

I took a good look at my challenger and had to admit
she was better at me than me—floppier hat, rimmed
with profusions of bright blooms; periwinkle blouse
rhymed perfectly to her eyes.

And those widening pupils that tunneled down
like the black holes artists render at the centers
of galaxies. I had to hold fast to my chair
to keep from sliding in.

WITH APOLOGIES TO STEPHEN HAWKING

Why do we remember the past but not the future?

~ Stephen Hawking

On the corner of a strange town—
clapboard house, unkempt lawn

porthole window in the peeling door
A place I know well   But shouldn't

From a dream? Or that other time
when I knew myself to be someone else?

Or what oddly seems more likely—the further one
I will breathe into later   I know

what you want to say
I shouldn't trust this

There are roundabouts in the brain
to account for déjà vus—the confluence

of synapses that sometimes make
the foreign   strangely familiar

and you're sure
to assure me that the mind

and we in its carriage are confined
to a singular direction   The Past

in its rattling pursuit of Future

Not even you, Stephen Hawking,
with your magnificently folded

and matterful gray, thought you could
remember the future   and yet

          Here we are

THE SKIES OF THE 50S

When the astronomer darkens
the dome of the Rose Planetarium
to coax out the stars, there's no
stopping them. Each deepening
of the dark brings more
until we're buried
in an avalanche of stars... stars
upon stars—a nearly total eclipse
of all we'd taken for true.

The astronomer breaks through
from his lectern: *These...*
before the stampede of electric lamps
eroded our nights... These
were the skies of the 1950s.

And we're on the ground again.
Count us among the fallen
in the great wars between wonder
and grief—spread-eagle
on the threadbare grasses of childhood,
clinging to our bright little beachball
splashing through the unfathomable
as it flops with stars.

BACK WHEN THE WORLD WAS ROUND

Trees, raindrops, and pebbles spoke
in rings. Poets and their poems, girls
and their gossips, sages and their secrets
traveled in circles. Even the great turtle
took the curved path—spiraled down
through the seasons and hours, down

through the years. I don't know how
we came to this flattening of time—
the pulping and pressing of trees
into calendars, the sad taming of the dervish
clock who once spread his luminous hands
in our kitchens and whirled.

Those digital footmen have carried him off
over the cliffs of our smartphones
and bedside tables, leaving us
homesick and bewildered, exiles
on this great pilgrimage, on the long curving
potholed path from here to here.

SOLVE FOR X

If x equals 2y plus or minus zero,
and y is the secret the sycamores keep
in their wintering roots or the sudden trill
of the redwing blackbird... or y is
the purpled light you see sometimes
with your eyes closed...

Or let y be the storm-track that rattles
the lonely traveler, the distant voice
that calls in an oddly familiar language
you can't quite make out. Regardless

of the shape y takes, you will need two.
You will need to open both top and bottom
dutch doors, empty both chambers:
Double the room in your heart.

Then it is yours to invite them in—
those Elysian y's.
Assure them as their host
that for your part
you will add nothing,
take nothing away.

MATTERS OF SCALE

Some days I have the heart
of a hungry ghost—nothing
in this world can fill it.

But each of today's citizenry
have become so vast
I can't contain a single one.

Dragonflies and tree frogs, the tiny
blossoms they call shooting stars—
all peer in at me with piercing
immeasurable eyes.

RELATIVE VELOCITY

I don't have forever, my friend
who was in need of a lover
told God... *like You do.*

Her garden was overgrown,
breakfast nook empty, feet
interminably cold. That's the way
it is down here where leaf-blowers
cough up dust devils and possums
ginger forth at dusk to stare in
with troubled pink eyes.

In these parts it's one
perplexing whirl from this to that.
She didn't need money she said or
a place to rest her head. She had enough
of just about everything.

But Time was something else and though
she reasoned that the Eternal
didn't have much use for it, Time
was the only train in town. So she boarded
the milk-run and sent up her plea and

just like that a good-looking fisherman
blew into the yard sale—no projects
of his own (as specified)—
just an easy smile, warm feet,
and an almost unearthly eagerness
to get things done.

QUANTUM ENTANGLEMENT

The animals who dare
come close… harbor seal,
Guernsey at the fence,
semi-feral cat…

It's no small thing for them,
I think, to brave the smell of thought.

Nose to nose—as we are now—
they look so familiar.

Who is it that lives in there?
Some part of me that wandered off
and has circled back
    to startle the living
        back in?

RUDIMENTS

All I need to make a comedy
is a park, a policeman,
and a pretty girl.

~ Charlie Chaplin

For the Blues: one sad heap of every shattered thing—
     the window, the promise, an uprising of springs
          set loose from the unsprung heart.

For a Torch Song: cobalt sequins, unquenchable sea.
     Brown-edged gardenia   fragrant as sorrow
          broke loose from her hair.

For a Country Tune: a 3-legged dog, a dollar-store
     ring, and one garden-variety perennial
          no-good cheatin' heart.

For a Sea Chantey: shipmates lost to the anarchies
     of wind. Inebriated clouds. The captain's
          heavy limp.   Glory
               of fish in the air.

For a Lullaby: start with a muskrat and a river.
     Shove the muskrat off in his blue-bottomed dinghy.
          Toss him an umbrella of stars.

THE UNTEACHABLE MOMENT

You don't need to teach a child to fall in love
with the wild patch at the end of the road—heady
with frog bleep and creek burble, the smell
of earthworms and decaying moss.
Every child knows that pussy willows
and spring mud are calls to prayer.

Under the yellow-green breeze-rippled
dome everything wriggles forth
to be baptized: Chipmunk and salamander.
Robin, tadpole, water skater, bee.

The Earth doesn't need to be taught
to love her child; she'll pull out the stops
for that joy-smudged face—scribble
on river rocks and tumble them downstream,
call on the sun's rays to cakewalk
on water.   She'll dangle vines
for her children to grab hold
        and fly
over the brook as it rages with rain.

II

charaiveti
charaiveti

SEAFARERS

We come to love the heron
for his artful tucking-in of tribulations,
the morning cloud for her coolheaded
midwifery of the sun.

We are grateful for the way the sea
goes gray in tune with the sky.
Nothing more asked of us—
neither from above nor below.

For the way the ship moves
like a sage through the narrows,
its engines grinding: *Charaiveti, charaiveti...*
Keep going, its only song.

We see it briefly now—we never were
the passenger. Nor are we the ship.
Only this flux and flow, a conjuring—
the oscillation of sunlight on sea.

THE SCENT OF JASMINE

a contrapuntal*

in India I found	if nothing else
cowbell clangor persists	life remains peculiar
it will haunt you	in the end a life
clanking with joy	is laid bare
dizzy with morning	all roads lead
jasmine-scented	to where we are going
beyond the gate	in the midst of birth and
in his tattered turban and lungi	death
the watcher stands guard as	we are dismantled
translucent as hunger	at last we give in to the pull
and the thirst	that gathers the love
in the alabaster eye	of this great dark storm

* *to be read horizontally & vertically / 3 ways*

ELEPHANT

From the rickshaw in Mumbai
we gasped when we saw her—
haphazardly heaped with sticks & straw
nearly double her size,
dripping with afternoon light.
Her driver rocked on the rippling gray
sea of her, a skinny turbaned silhouette
against the gold.

I think I rode an elephant once—
or was it only a dream?
Climbing the ladder with my two
girls, sitting astride her broad
carpeted back. I can still feel her
pitching beneath us as we clung
to the braided fringe and she bumbled
along her frayed & dusty track.

But mostly I remember the top
of her head: a few hairs rising
from between fluid ears,
a mostly bald dome—vulnerable,
like an elder who's given her all.
Surrendered now:
    I'll go where you lead.
       I'll rest in your shade.
           I'll carry what you give.

HOW TO BEFRIEND UNCERTAINTY

Come sit in the seat by the window—
near the birds who have shaken off
their dreams and opened themselves
to this never-to-be-again day.

Today we won't be asked
to bumble along the beaten byways,
for Uncertainty is our houseguest.
Put on the water,
set out the homemade jam.

Uncertainty will listen with us
as our bagels pop
from the toaster's dark mouth
and the coffee grounds weep
their bittersweet sobs.

Uncertainty is Mystery's love child—
no history, no proper name—
but she has always been with us.

She is the one who wakes us
to drizzle new questions into our day,
new stories, new colors and light.

The wind is her breath.
Her body is the water
we bathe in and drink.

Uncertainty, with her barefoot-dancing
gypsy soul knows the unpaved roads
to gratitude by heart.

But of certain things—like tomorrow—
she knows nothing.

And because of this,
her love knows no bounds.

PUCCINI PLAYS ON TURTLE ISLAND

This morning I cleaned house and did laundry—
the underwear drawer well-stocked and tidy again.
Then it was my favorite path—through the woods
and into the used bookstore, on to the corner
café and home again where my sweetheart
bakes bread and has put on opera—arias
from the deep, perhaps the very same deep
the wild-eyed woman on the cliffs of Mendocino
told me she was trying to find her way out of.
Outside, the bird feeder is full. The cold trough
continues to push down from Alaska, keeping
the pear tree's buds closed in on themselves,
lost in thought. The gray world out the window
is at peace with herself, even as she knows
the atmospheric river will continue to wash
all her loves downstream. What's left
of my friends have scattered—Italy, Costa Rica,
the Otherworld, Japan. It seems I am meant
to sit still in this well-swept house—
in this eye of turbulent absence. It comes clear
that no one can save us from falling
from the edge. And now I think maybe
we are ferried on the back of a great turtle after all—
a tottering benevolent beast, content with time
and its machinations, content
to paddle over the channels of dark matter,
to hobble across the starry way.

HEADING FOR ALASKA

I didn't know I was wanting
wilderness, but it seems she'd
been wanting me. Already—the forest
deepening beyond the shuttle window
plies her highway robbery,
snatches my trappings away.

> *... how personally I'd taken*
> *my losses... how fiercely*
> *I'd clung to my own little*
> *torn and bandaged moon...*

Now there are ancient boulders
along the highway, wind
in the upper branches. The grasses
toss their ghostly wishes out
over the path. Stands
of sycamore shamelessly weep.

BANDELIER, NEW MEXICO

Everyone needs to spend a little
time in the high desert where
on cloudless nights you can stand
at the edge of the woven worlds
and take in the space between thoughts—
where you can look through
the moth-eaten quilt of the sky
and come to know stars
as the raised glasses of the ancestors
in love-stricken pause
before toasting us—their children's
children's children—their faceted goblets
glinting as puzzles of light.

LINES WRITTEN ON THE TRAIL WITH MY NOTE-TAKING APP

It's time you took a more senior role he told me though I'm not
exactly sure what that means except maybe to drift back get
out of the way leave the plot & its machinations to the up and
comings and follow the lonesome trail which is where you'd
find me now if you were looking though I wouldn't blame you
if you weren't and even if you were it's a pretty remote trail and
the chance of us meeting is almost zilch which is why I decided
to type this on my phone to you but more to the point is the
question of who exactly you are the one I seem to call out to
when I'm alone like this though I'm beginning to suspect that
the one I'm addressing is very likely none other than some feral
version of myself—Hobbit woman, trollish valley-dweller, one
of wide feet & messy demeanor & sentimental persuasion, the
kind who might find in her Neanderthal-Lineage-Self the simple
decency to bury her dead friends with flowers... but what really
gets me as I type this as I flail around for words to describe such
an astronomically one-of-a-kind moment in the great expanse
is how the note-taking app I'm using to write this is so good at
coming up with my next word... more often than not, the whole
dang phrase.

THE GAME OF HEARTS

Your job is to lose
as many tricks as possible
so when the cards are laid
on the table, you come up empty.

You'll want whatever sweetness
you've been dealt
to wind up in somebody else's hand.
Strangely winning logic—the art
of giveaway, of lying low.

It is wise to make peace with the dark—
especially the lady who holds it in spades,
whose heavy heart will surely topple
the endgame scales. Know
where she lives—the Pariah Queen—
and whenever you can, set her free.

But if you find she's slunk
into your lair… Oh well. For just this
one round give up the ghost, give in
to the underground broodings of soul.
Go the whole hog. Shoot the moon.

20TH ANNIVERSARY

Could this be the love poem
where I get to walk through
the bakery door again and you
get to hope I'm the one—

the one you've been writing to for weeks?
Isn't that the pewter sky of January,
the pungence of coffee wafting up
from chipped white diner mugs?

The downtown trees have seen it all;
they go on with their town-square
gossips. The pigeons show more interest,
tuned as they are to crumble of muffin

and scone. But even they don't notice
our snow-capped selves, hunched
outside to eavesdrop on the scene,
looking in through the steamed-up windows.

Your eyes are beautiful, you say.
I'd like to see you again.
But not out loud.
You wait to go home
and write it in a letter.

MOTHER, BEGINNINGS...

Mother as wind-struck lake
as whirling dervish cottonwood

Mother in the Sylvania's
blue light, stainless
bowl of popcorn, frothing
mug of beer

Mother running naked/ father
fallen from the roof

Mother as banging screen door
Mother as rain

Mother as shapeshifting
shadow over hedges
and walls

*   *   *

Up here on the lookout
over what she's christened
God's Country she fixes
her gaze soothsayer-hard

You can circle the Earth
a thousand times she says
but nothing will strike
truer than this

*   *   *

Mother as wishing well
as uncaged bird

Mother as a window in the stairwell
small square of moonlight
and a silver spoon

Mother as Neanderthal bones
discovered with needle
and thread
flowers for homage
a small reed flute

Mother as the question
no one thought to ask
a menagerie of salt
dissolving in the sea

WHAT RAINS

—half a sestina

When the French composer Satie died
they found 200 umbrellas in his flat,
maybe to keep the penciled notes from washing away
in the grief-storms that howled under his roof.
In any case, his music came out wet—the strings
welling up, falling over us like rain.

One long February it was snow that rained
into my life—a blizzard of innocence in the dead
of winter. Enough to loosen the taut strings
of my teenage daughters' hearts (their wonder flat
and dark, disappointment-drenched from toe to roof.)
But that day we let the snow wash us away

down to the Niagara, whose icy thunder washed away
the years. I watched them grow young again under a rain
of colored stars that shimmered over the rooftops—
a storm of fireworks reflected on snow. I could have died
right there, seeing them so alive, so silly, so flat-
out happy, dancing like puppets released from their strings.

HOUSE

I had one once—in Maine. An almost-ancient farmhouse
with a chicken coop and fruit trees and a clothesline
you could use if the dryer was broke, which it was
most winters. The bedsheets and pajamas froze stiff
in the frigid sun, but once you brought them in
they'd thaw like a miracle and dry just as quick.

There were always more than enough eggs
and sugar peas and afternoons—in the kitchen
where the brick bread-oven had been plastered over,
in the forties we figured, when everybody wanted
things smoothed-over.   Not us.

We chipped away at it—the whole house.
Tore off the drywall, sledge-hammered the ceiling.
We had at it till the bricks in the kitchen shone
and unfinished beams in the front room gave
the impression of sitting in the ribcage of a whale.
We bored through the outer walls of that room
to put in a second hearth. We burned it all up
there—the inheritance money and our marriage.
But it was Maine and in those latitudes
you're grateful for anything warm.

WINTER SOLSTICE

The year finally catches her tail
and sleeps   her bleary breath
lures melancholy
     up from the hollows below

She crosses the room
stands at the window   looks out

Something like kindness
washes her face
She's not much of a talker
No tall tale   No complaint

You put on the water for tea

MOBIUS STRIP

for Abhi

Things taste different now, she tells me, now
that she has taken death as her paramour.

A strange foreverness
        keeps getting into it all.

Each forkful of cake holds the bittersweet
of all the devil's food her tongue has touched.

The dew of each morning is wet
with the newness of every dawn.

When she grieves now, she's back
in the marshes where all it took was a single

step for ten thousand sorrows to flare up
        as snow geese
                and whirl—

a stunning chaos that left the world
        stuttering
                wild and white.

3 A.M.

living alone you wake
sometimes
under the high ceilings
      potted jades and violets
      the Buddha's burnished face
      beneath his paper shade
and wonder
about the one who lives here
      how she counts
      and colors her days
you're touched
by her considered placement
of things   a tenderness
you keep in your heart
for strangers

A DAY

You open the day, and look—
a sack of what you've always wanted
has been dropped at your door: sunlit hours
with lizards crawling through them.
The frog pond's improvisational chorus
of croak and plop. Redwoods inch up
towards tomorrow, and the stream
where you decide to rest,
though diminished in dry season,
gurgles ever-so-faintly on.

MORNING ON THE TRAIL

One of the camp counselors
is scribbling cryptic notes
to slip between layers
of honey mushrooms
or inside the little tents
she's pitched
from moss and fallen
twigs—clues
for the lunchtime
scavenger hunt. And for one
dizzying moment
I'm all but certain
that's me over there,
crouched in my
goldfinch and peach blossom
dress, in the waterfall
body of my youth—
the hunt
about to begin.

NERUDA'S ABANDONED STUDY

Not so different from the old poet, I think,
as I look through the silvered haze of his room.
Light sifts in through the crocheted curtains.
Wooden figures colonize the desk—ships in bottles,
children on a swing. One sad frog.
Wilted flowers mark time beside the brass lamp
overcome with dust.

He is not writing. His poems have flown—
have been spirited away, out beyond the path
with its blackberries and rabbits.
He has gone on with them—
broken open as he is—
bat-blind, soaring through the dark,
baying his tender mournful cries,
clear and generous as rain.

DIVINE CONTAGION

The back stoop loves summer
for her alternating currents
of gardenia and mint

The gate loves the evening
and its winds

The children love the gate's creak—
winter's grumpiness caught in the hinge

The brook loves the salamander
for its wriggling—in and out

The salamander loves the boy
who spoke in tender mumbles
before he let her go

The evening star loves the dark
for bringing out her light
Every citizen of heaven loves all
that gleams black—beak of raven
                    mongoose tail
                              burrow of mole

The nearly invisible clothes moth loves
her unequivocal mission—
                    to loosen the weave

LEAVING MENDOCINO

There's nothing we can do
about the rogue wave of sadness
that nips at the heels of our happiest days.

On one visit, you wrote the good part
of a play; another, I painted
a brown bear's face.

This time it was ravens.
You sketched them from the picnic bench
as they rode the updrafts
and *cukalooed* across the cliffs.

The only way home now
is to steer the switchbacks—
their yellowed fields
and stands of sycamore
hung with moss.

It's a fog-banked Route One.
Late summer.
The pewter rim of the year
glints dim through the haze
as we dip together into the dark.

Once in a while a bird flits
through our sadness—turkey vultures
and hummers. Fence posts, dairy cows,
and fishermen in knee-high boots
dragging buckets home.

A little later, almost without notice,
it will break. The way storms do
and renegade prisoners
and everything else.

But first, we must navigate the known—
these black butterflies and apparitions,
the cold pull of sorrow at our feet.

THE MYSTERY SCHOOL OF RHYME

Tell me it ain't monumental; tell me it's just accidental:
    rapture, capture
        womb and tomb
            ease and trees, trees and breeze
    try, cry, lie, die...
        all the notes on the road to why.

Tell me you're not stoked when your words come unchoked:
    Curl and unfurl
        swirl and twirl
            like the tail of a squirrel
like the stories of a girl.

Did you see her as she fell
        into that sacred spell— ?
            that spell made of rhymes
that spell so sublime
    it throws you out of time.

1-2-3-4-5-6-7: this is where heaven
    begins to leaven.
        Understand what I'm sayin'?
        Listen to this rain
And tell me it's not prayin'.

III

pitcher of twilight
angel of glass

SLEEPING WITH THE RAVENS

All night they flapped through me
on blue-black wings. By morning
every hair on my head had gone white

and was risen. Like wayward roots
they burrowed into the firmament.

I woke with that old raw
hunger… ravenous.

Not for starlight
but for what recedes—
the bottomless yearning

to walk with the ancient novitiates
who carry white fire
in their cupped dark hands.

IN THE TEMPLE OF SAD GOODBYES

When sadness sat at my table   last night
I saw that he was beautiful   just like my friend
told me he was   the friend who called
last week to tell me   she was dying

Beautiful sadness   windows
smudged with steam   the ceaseless watercourse way
the vanishing   of all who consent to radiate light

melancholy night   filled with rain

DUENDE'S MISTRESS SPEAKS

Don't talk to me about sorrow.
I winter with her in the weeping
groves. I crush her dark leaves
and drink them for breakfast.

We commiserate in the lost tongues
of wolfhound and crow—
dialects sour as vinegar,
bitter as stone.

Gilded in heartbreak, sorrow
and I slip in sideways,
slap the naked ground
with our broad bare feet.

Ours is the sizzle of the arrow
in flight.   In winter our exhales
take the shape
        of small white birds.

MY FATHER DIES AGAIN, FORTY YEARS LATER

The hospital is a border town
where locals braid their last straws
round their fingers as they sit
on the stoops to sing.

In the next life let me rise, she sings,
the one with bandaged eyes.
Like a seabird, let me fly!

Further down, a mime in pajamas
teeters through a hallway of honey.
This is when my whisper of a father
slips out through the body's hidden hatch.

The room goes white—a crystal palace,
a salt mine, brilliant and cool, a cavern
made by the hidden rush
        of underground streams.

IS THAT YOU IN THE WIND?

If I sit very still
it seems I can hear you
whistling through the house again,
like you did up the stairs
when happiness blew through
for no reason.

NOT IN OUR HANDS

for Elianne awaiting final passage

It's not in our hands—the woods
grow dense with underbrush and spruce
and filaments of lightning leap down
to set the world on fire.

The valley fills with smoke, thick
as white mustard; the mountain
steps back to veil her face.

It's not up to us who draws near,
or when—caribou, moose,
horseshoe rabbit, bear.
But the one we need, in its own time comes.
Raven woke us every dawn
in Juneau, and after you and I had said
our last goodbye, Eagle drew close
as a breath, then up and away.

From the boat—a bear foraged along the edge,
and from the train home, a sad-eyed moose—
its antlers drizzled with grass and mud.

These visitors have prepared me for the winds
that come to tear me open now,
so you can sail through—clear
though me—to the other shore.

THINNING OF THE VEIL

I should have known it was a dream
when the 16-wheeler I was driving bent
like Silly Putty to allow for the U-turn
on that narrow country road. Or

when the harbor seal left the shore
to come with me over the dunes, upright,
somehow, with the blue-eyed swagger
of my now-dead brother.

It's easy from this side to sort for reason.
But in those parts the drape between worlds is less
like the heavy velvet dropped between scenes,
more like the bridal veil that only casts a mist
over the eyes of the bride so it's impossible
to miss how intently they're fixed on you.

PRAISE IN DARK TIMES

Praise the sorrow that took us out in the night—
the cold snap of wind in her sails
Praise the king tides that spilled us
      onto the shore of this difficult day

Praise the mystery that rises when the ground gives way
Praise the toppling of arrogant men cast in bronze
Praise the night and what we cannot see
      Praise all that is dark

Praise all the Black boys and girls
with hearts as big as Africa
Bless their soul-deep eyes
and the songs the earth gave them
      to sing

Bless their singing as it enters us
Bless the singing earth as she enters us
Bless her sacred songs
      in all the forgotten keys

DAY OF DISTANCING

Enter the ways of morning, the body
of morning—the waking of bee and leaf,
spider and newt. The way morning sun catches
in the threads that ferry thoughts
between the trees, visible only in this light.

Have you noticed how, when we finally let go,
all we've ever wanted comes?
By which I mean love—not the come-and-go,
flare-and-fade kind, but love as a cloud of gnats
you can walk through, or as the kingfisher's
impossible stillness on his branch above the lake.

How did we come to think we had no time for this?

These days seem mostly to give us ourselves,
over and over… happy to take us, to break us open—
wider, deeper and more true.

My grandsons want to visit—all four of them, strong
and singular as the four directions. And my sable-skinned
granddaughter—queen of the night. I want
to take each one in my arms. Oh, what the hell,
I say when no one is listening, let me die of hugging.

But instead I stay inside and hold them
here—distanced and masked.

Most things are smaller now, except for what's big—
like when our hearts break each day and set loose
the strands the weavers will use in the night—
threading them at lake's edge to catch the morning light.

FEVER

The fortress goes to mud
and the moonstruck exiles return—
legions of luminous strangers
come to overthrow the crown.

At turns you're eye to eye
with house wren and angel,
phantom and flower.

Through the double-hung window
the sky falls away and the pear tree
blossoms into prayer.

Like ants finding honey, love
steals into everything. You weep
when the breezes shudder the finch
and later when the sun turns
her copper gaze to the mountain.

Even the dead won't keep their distance.
They hold the cup when you pour the tea,
fly with you into the pasture on the hill.

For these many days nothing will get done.
Except in the old Taoist way—when
the ancient ones did nothing and nothing
was left undone.

IN THE BARDO'S AVIARY

In the mudroom on a nest woven
from the fallen—feathers, pine needles,
tattered bits of floss—she sits
and warms her green-speckled eggs.
One filled with lightning, one
with wind. One with a hairline crack
through which we barely see
a tiny dark eye.

Fish flash around her
bright and sudden as stars.
They leap from the countless corners
of Indra's net—an infinite regress
of worlds within worlds—every one alive
with morning and salt.

LIKE THE BARNS IN RURAL MAINE

In the obituaries & at the memorials the story
is all accolades & affections. *Put her
on a crosstown bus*, they'll say, *and she'll
come home with 10 new friends.*

Nobody but the deceased can speak
for the loneliness that hung its coat in the foyer,
wandered the house at night, put away
the dishes when the guests had gone.

In the end we only see the front page
of a life. Like the barns in rural Maine,
the side that faces the road is the only one
to get the paint. Behind it, on the inside

is where the losses are piled in bales,
held together with twine. Unanswered
questions gape like leaky roof boards, doubts
cling to the rafters like bats.

We have come to celebrate a life—
a bucket of light that churned with grief,
disappointments nibbling at the ankles
like no-see-ums. Nobody taught us

how to celebrate those parts—the bigger
hungrier parts each of us surreptitiously
shift from shoulder to shoulder, hip to hip,
as we slosh face-first down the road.

IN THE COUNTING HOUSE

Before they did the assignment they always asked if it was going
to count.
And if it counted, they wanted to know how much it would
count.

I cleaned for a millionaire who owned two mansions—one with
a 30-foot
waterfall, one in a lakeside stand of pines, but she always made
me count

out two dollars in coin before she'd give me the fifty-dollar bill.
She held her breath and her empty outstretched hand as I counted.

They tell me once it was tulip bulbs. Before that, shells
and beads and hand-carved figurines is what we'd count.

Who was happier—the king in his counting house? Or his queen
with bread and honey—a sweetness he could count on?

Some days it amounts to almost nothing, my little
stash of this & that... but who's counting?

Yes, worries cheep at the window, Prartho, but turn and see how rich
the birds at their feeder, seeds flying like flung stars—too many
to count.

PERSONAL EFFECTS

I'd make a terrible scout, jangling along as I do—
this xylophone of stones and bones.   I travel heavy

and clamorous. What with all the extra pockets tailors
have sewn in for my noisy assets of river rocks
and shells, not to mention the bagpipes of digestion
and breath, the bamboo clack of weary bones…

I was hoping in the flyaway world such effects
would weigh me down. But that seems ever less

likely. So, when my end comes and you sorters
turn to one another to ask, *What does she have
in these boxes?   Rocks?*

All that will be left for you
          is to smile.

EMPTYING THE BOAT

I begin to see what I've come to give:
the empty part, the part I took for useless,
the shell the losses scrubbed clean.

My work is to empty the boat
so when you sail me out
over the glinting mystery
there'll be room for my song to roll around
and echo back to shore—part sob,
part howl, part foghorn wail.

My work is to practice being wind-borne,
to give myself up to the air, to be lifted
on the westerlies and poured back
over the earth, like rain.

AUTUMN ACCOUNTS

They say it's never too late, what with
George HW's skydive for his 90th
and the hundred-year-old water skier
who bobbed and waved from my fridge
till his photo yellowed and frayed.

But it probably is too late to become
a rocket scientist or oral surgeon, too late
to free climb Half Dome or perform as
the principal in Swan Lake.
And it's surely too late to die young.

Still, there may be time
to enter the longing and give ourselves
to what we become
when we turn in its light:

Pitcher of twilight,
    angel of glass,
        a grasshopper the size
            of a young boy's heart.

A labyrinth of stones, like the one
    we discovered in the hills—
        that slow-walk to nowhere,

the very same nowhere
    we were getting to
        so fast.

PRACTICE RUN

We get a few practice runs. One day,
for instance, as your plane lifts off your life
passes before you, the city below strewn
with spent days—at once devastating
and beautiful when spread out this way—
the potholed landscape of catastrophe & grace.

You'll feel like the bricklayer watching the weather
take down the walls, the gardener at the fence after harvest,
the conductor at the window of his emptied train.

You'll see the good bits were small but everywhere—
fine threads worked into a coarse weave. You'll see
what an immensity it's been to walk & breathe &
feel things for which there are no words.

You'll wonder how you missed
the tenderness of the breezes in your leaves.

You'll wish you'd done almost everything
differently.   Then again
would you really change a thing?

THE TEMPLE MASTER TAKES HIS LEAVE

the elegant pitcher falls

emptiness

everywhere

*   *   *   *

how quiet
         the water
                  just before boiling

*   *   *   *

You have carved me out
so deeply
soon I'll be able
to swallow the sky.

*   *   *   *

a well-cleaned fruit seed
falls on the page

is that you
in the trees
savoring the cherries?

*   *   *   *

now
all
my
questions
will
be
pebbles
dropped
into
a
bottomless
well:

not

one

plunk

NOTES

Many of the poems in this collection, especially those in the first section, bear titles and various interior details borrowed from physics, astronomy, mathematics, and other technologies. These references are used metaphorically in the exploration of everyday contemporary life. Along with other relevant backstories, a good portion of the following notes comprise a brief glossary of technical terms or references, created to the best of my capacities. Apologies to experts in these fields for any misunderstandings.

* The book's epigraph is from Maria Popova's essay collection *Figuring*, and is used here with permission from the author.

* *Table of Correspondences* is a term from esoteric philosophy, referring to a comparative list of properties in different systems, which are analogous or have affinity with each other.

* *Temple*: The poem refers to the stones of the deconstructed Santa Maria de Óvila monastery, built in Spain in 1181 and purchased by William Randolph Hearst in the 1920s, which he shipped to the US with the idea of incorporating them into a personal dwelling in California. But Hearst ran out of money before architects could finish the design, and he eventually gifted the stones to the City of San Francisco. In the early 1940s, it was decided to rebuild the monastery in Golden Gate Park and make it a museum of medieval art. But a series of fires in the 1940s and 1950s ultimately made putting the monastery back together impossible.

For years, many of the stones were left in heaps behind the Japanese Tea Garden, some of them moved about the park (and even taken home) by workers and visitors.

In 1965, the church portal, which had been in a separate warehouse from the damaging fires, was reassembled and became part of an entrance to the de Young Museum in Golden Gate Park. When the de Young was demolished and rebuilt in 2002, the portal was donated to the University of San Francisco, who used it to grace the Kalmanovitz Amphitheater.

In 2013, the chapter house was successfully rebuilt at the Abbey of New Clairvaux in Vina, California, using about two-thirds of the original stones.

* *Diagramming the Sentence* refers to the fading academic art of charting a sentence's parts of speech and their relationships to one another.

The simplest sentences consist of a **predicate** (verb) and its **subject** (the person, thing, or idea that "acts" through the verb). The subject is sometimes merely "understood," as in "Run!" A sentence's **object** indicates what the subject acts upon.

A **relative clause** is a type of dependent clause with its own subject and verb, but which can't stand alone as a sentence.

A **split infinitive** occurs when a modifier (e.g., an adverb) breaks up the two parts of an infinitive verb (a verb with the preposition "to"). This has been considered a grammatical error, though less so in modern usage.

A **dangling participle** is an adjective that is unintentionally modifying the wrong noun in a sentence because it is too far away from its subject.

* *Mirrored Palace*: In Einstein's theory of relativity—the **gravitational bending of light**, is the now-verified idea that light curves when it moves through space distorted by gravity.

The "incalculable darknesses" refer to **dark matter**, a hypothetical form of matter thought to account for approximately 85% of the matter in the universe and which is completely invisible. It emits no light or energy and thus cannot be detected by conventional sensors and detectors.

The "great thinkers" who saw fairies include Sir Arthur Conan Doyle, creator of Sherlock Holmes.

The "nanoscopic dot" is the single, nascent, super-dense particle imagined to contain everything, which, according to the **Big Bang Theory**, exploded and released all we know, are yet to know, and all that will remain unknown into existence.

* *Vanishing Point*: A **Vanishing Point** is the point at which receding parallel lines viewed in perspective appear to converge; finding and staying true to this point is an essential step in perspective drawing.

* *Event Horizons*: An **Event Horizon** is a theoretical boundary around a black hole beyond which no light or other radiation can escape; i.e., a point of no return.

* *Negative Capability*: **Negative Capability** is a writer's ability, "which Shakespeare possessed so enormously," to accept "uncertainties, mysteries, doubts, without any irritable reaching after fact and reason," as created and defined by the English poet John Keats in an 1817 letter. In science, negative capability can refer to the negative pole of an electric current, where the passive and receptive negative pole is capable of receiving current from the positive pole.

* *The Butterfly Effect*: **The Butterfly Effect** is an aspect of Chaos Theory whereby a minute localized change in a complex system can have large effects elsewhere. The hypothetical example that gives this phenomenon its name is the flutter of a butterfly's wings in Nebraska, which as it travels and changes could, in due course, cause a sand storm in the Sahara Desert.

* *Particles & Waves*: In 1905, the 26-year-old Albert Einstein proposed the paradox that light could be both wave and particle, **Particles** being the building blocks of matter, confined to a tiny space, while **Waves** are defined as disturbances or variations in a medium that transfer energy progressively, spreading from point to point.

Most recently, Quantum Theorists have proposed a unification theory, not only for light, but for all phenomena, stating that in reality all objects are waves, though in some approximations the wave might look like a moving ball… or a lemon tree's first fruit; i.e. a particle.

* *With Apologies to Stephen Hawking*: Whenever I hear Hawking ask why we don't remember the future, I silently (and affectionately) quip to his ghost, "Speak for yourself, Stephen!"

* *The Skies of the 50s*: This poem describes an experience at the Rose Planetarium in New York City contrasted against childhood memories of stargazing in the 1950s. It refers to the sad phenomena known as **erosion of the night**—the diminishment of visible stars due to man-made light pollution. In a 2016 study for *Science Advances*, an international team of researchers created a detailed atlas of light pollution around the world, leading them to estimate that the Milky Way is no longer visible to fully one-third of humanity—including 60 percent of Europeans and 80 percent of Americans.

* *Back When the World Was Round* explores ideas about **The Circle** through time. Early sciences, particularly geometry and astronomy, were inextricably interwoven with ideas about the divine. Early scientists of these disciplines believed that there was something intrinsically divine to be found in circles.

* *Solve for X* plays with "solving" the basic algebraic equation, with a nod to the strangeness of zero, which, because of its unique property of being neither positive nor negative, can be given or taken without changing the result.

* *Matters of Scale*: **The Hungry Ghost** refers to a concept in Buddhism where one constantly seeks something outside oneself to curb an insatiable yearning for relief or fulfillment.

* *Relative Velocity*: **Relative Velocity** is the velocity (speed in a given direction) of an object with respect to its observer. (It gets more complicated than that, but essentially we are considering the *apparent* speed of another as various factors change in the observer and the observed.)

* *Quantum Entanglement*: **Quantum Entanglement** relates to the observation that aspects of one particle in an *entangled pair* depend on aspects of the other particle—no matter how far apart they are or what lies between them.

* *Seafarers*: **Charaiveti, Charaiveti** is a Sanskrit phrase that means "keep going." Its origins are ancient, appearing in the *Aitareya-Upanishad* (circa 6th or 5th century BCE): "Honeybees move constantly to give honey, birds keep flying and the sun is perpetually emitting light...CHARAIVETI, CHARAIVETI." Gautama Buddha is said to have ended his sermons with this counsel.

* *The Scent of Jasmine*: **Contrapuntal** is a musical term involving counterpoint, in which more than one musical line plays at the same time, with lines that are independent but harmonically related.

* *How to Befriend Uncertainty* was written as an example poem for 6th graders while I taught as a Poet-in-the-Schools on Zoom during Covid 19 lockdown. Right before class, I followed my own assignment, which was to give advice that would be helpful to myself during those strange stay-at-home days. Details I asked my students (& myself) to include:
1. Imperatives — Short & clear directive statements
2. Negatives — Include what is NOT there or what NOT to do
3. An IF statement — Tell us what to do IF... (something strange) happens
4. Sensory Detail — Include colors, sounds, tastes, smells, textures
5. Surprise Yourself! Be a little wild.

* *Puccini Plays on Turtle Island*: In various Indigenous creation stories, the turtle is said to support the world, the land we live on together sometimes referred to as **Turtle Island**.

* *Bandelier, New Mexico* is one of the high deserts in the United States where the Milky Way can still be seen in its full glory.

* *Lines Written on the Trail with my Note-Taking App*: Though this poem easily relates to experiences with ChatGPT and other AI writing programs, when I wrote it on my iPhone, I hadn't discovered these yet. This poem was created using the pre-loaded note-taking app on my iPhone, to which I made only a few small tweaks for the final version.

* *The Game of Hearts*: This is my precise strategy for the card game I spent many rainy days playing with my siblings. It is a game played in tricks, where the only cards that garner points are the hearts (one point each), and the queen of spades (worth 13). **Shooting the Moon** is a round where one player takes all the pointed cards, which reverts those points to each of the other players. The player with the lowest score wins.

The **Endgame Scales** refer to the Egyptian myth where the deceased's heart is weighed on a scale against Ma'at's feather of truth before entering the Afterlife. Only if the heart balances with the feather, can the soul continue on her journey.

* *What Rains*: This is actually 1 and 1/2 lines short of half a **Sestina**—a French form of poetry consisting of six stanzas of six lines each and a final tercet of three lines. All stanzas have the same six

words at the end of the lines in six different sequences following a fixed pattern. The closing three-line envoi, which does not exist in this version (not even half of one), would contain all six words.

* *Möbius Strip* is an easily demonstrable mathematical concept of an infinite loop, which features a one-sided surface without boundaries. It can be created by taking a strip of paper, giving it an odd number of half-twists, then taping the ends back together to form a loop. If you take a pencil and draw a line along the center of the strip, the line will run along both sides of the loop.

* *A Day* was one of the poems in this collection written during the Covid 19 Pandemic lock-down, describing the unique texture of those days, which often included walks on neighborhood trails.

* *Neruda's Abandoned Study* was inspired by a photograph of one of Pablo Neruda's writing studios, taken shortly after his death.

* *The Mystery School of Rhyme* explores my suspicion that mystery teachings have been hidden in the sounds of words, particularly in words that "speak to one another" through rhyme. **Mystery Schools** have been formed since antiquity all over the globe in order to preserve & pass on the keys to living an enlightened and grace-filled life. These schools are composed of conclaves of initiates who dedicate themselves to the exploration and perpetuation of the *mystery teachings*.

* *Duende's Mistress Speaks*: The term **Duende**, a shortening of the phrase *Duen de Casa* (Master of the House), refers in Spanish culture to a trickster-spirit who makes a general nuisance of himself

by hiding things, breaking china, and making noise. The poet Federico Garcia Lorca, inspired by Andalusian nomad singers and dancers whom he witnessed being taken over by something mysterious, vast, and ancient, repurposed this idea as a measure of artistic depth. He describes the quality in his celebrated essay *In Search of Duende* (translation by A. S. Kline): "Those dark sounds are the mystery, the roots that cling to the mire that we all know, that we all ignore, but from which comes the very substance of art."

* *Praise in Dark Times*: Written in the aftermath of George Floyd's horrific murder, this poem reflects my desire to praise what dark times can sometimes bring. *The Black boys and girls with hearts as big as Africa* include and honor my five grandchildren.

* *Fever* was written during an illness that was diagnosed at Urgent Care in February 2020 as an "unknown virus." The virus wrestled me onto the living room couch where I lay with cough, fever, and exhaustion for more than a week and was sometimes visited by an all-encompassing sense of gratitude and love.

* *In the Bardo's Aviary*: In Tibetan Buddhism **The Bardo** is an intermediate state of existence between death and rebirth, during which one is given a direct experience of reality. The purity of the soul in transit determines her capacity to glean transcendental insight from this meeting with reality, perhaps even the ultimate liberation that is the soul's purpose through incarnations.

Indra's Net: an image from the Vedas and embraced by Mahayana Buddhism—a vast net of the god Indra, which stretches infinitely in all directions. At each juncture, in each "eye" of the net, is a single perfect jewel. Each jewel reflects every other jewel, infinite in number, and each of the reflected images of the jewels bears the image of all the other jewels—infinity to infinity. Thus, whatever affects one jewel affects them all.

Infinite Regress: a series of related elements with a first member but no last, where each element leads to the next in some sense. A concrete example from everyday life is when two or more parallel mirrors generate progressively smaller reflections that appear to continue through infinity.

* *In the Counting House* is a **Ghazal**, an Arabic poetic form written in couplets (two-line stanzas) where the first two lines end with the same word (or a variation on it). That refrain, then, continues to end each proceeding couplet. Unlike most European poetry, each couplet in a ghazal is able to stand alone, as if it were its own poem. (*Caveat*: In keeping with American Cowboy-Country tradition, two stanzas of my ghazal here are linked; i.e., unable to stand all that well on their own.) In a ghazal's last stanza, the poet addresses herself, inserting her own name in the first line of the final couplet.

Tulip Mania: The 1600s' Dutch tulip bulb market is one of the most famous asset bubbles and crashes of all time. At the height of the bubble, tulips sold for approximately 10,000 guilders, equal to the value of a mansion on the Amsterdam Grand Canal.

* *Practice Run* was written on a journey from Austin, Texas, to my home near the San Francisco Bay, with a brief change of planes in San Diego—a place I lived, on and off at different crisis points in my life, and where my daughters grew into adults and raised their

own families. It's a place I've visited scores of times for many decades, and when we lifted off—up over our various neighborhoods, beaches, parks, and celebration points, sweeping over those scattered dark corners where everything fell apart... well, this poem is my attempt to tell what I saw.

* *The Temple Master Takes His Leave*: These small verses were written in India in the first days after my spiritual master Osho left his body.

ACKNOWLEDGEMENTS

Grateful appreciation to the editors of the following journals and anthologies for first *curating** poems included in this collection, sometimes in slightly different versions:

Abandoned Mine: "Event Horizons" (also anthologized in the 2022 print version), "Starfall" [here as "Practice Run"], "Leaving Mendocino"

Bellevue Literary Review: "Fever"

California Poets in the Schools Anthology: "What Rains"

Chautauqua: "Puccini Plays on Turtle Island" (Pushcart nominated), "A Day"

Comstock Review: "Diagramming the Sentence," "Solve for X," "Duende's Mistress Speaks"

Conestoga Zen: "Matters of Scale," "Negative Capability"

Gyroscope Review: "Relative Velocity"

Last Stanza Poetry Journal: "Autumn Accounts," "Elephant," "Mother, Beginnings…," "Seafarers"

Love Poems, Vol. II: "Divine Contagion"

Marin Poetry Center Anthologies (2020, 21, &22): "House," "Morning on the Trail," "Rudiments"

Monterey Poetry Review: "Bandelier, New Mexico"

Osho News: "Not In Our Hands," "The Temple Master Takes His Leave," "The Unteachable Moment"

Pandemic Puzzle Poems: "Praise in Dark Times," "Day of Distancing," "How to Befriend Uncertainty"

Radical Teacher: "Chaos Theory" [here as "The Butterfly Effect"]

Rattle: "Charlie Chaplin & Me"

San Diego Annual (2020, 21, 22): "Neruda's Abandoned Study," "Sleeping with the Ravens," "20th Anniversary"

Stone Canoe: "Winter Solstice," "Table of Correspondences"

I would also like to thank my family and friends who not only persist in putting up with me, but supply the necessary inspiration from which these poems were cobbled. A special thanks goes to my writing partners—Kosrof Chantikian, for his fine-tuned ear and heart, and Catlyn Fendler, who prodded me to dig deeper, tell it wilder and more true, helping bring this manuscript to the best version of itself.

A heartfelt thank you to my publisher, the warm and wise Diane Frank, and my proof-readers Erik Ievins, Greg Goodridge, Anila Manning, Diana Donovan, and Catlyn Fendler.

And, as always, a nod of gratitude to each of my students, past, present, young, & seasoned, who continue to be among my wisest teachers.

---

* *Curate* is the new term suggested by Tim Green, editor-in-chief of the poetry journal *Rattle*, to replace "publish," in order to allow writing to be shared in blogs and on social media without being considered off-limits for first serial rights in the world of literary publications.

ABOUT THE AUTHOR

Prartho Sereno has made her home in a bamboo hut in India, a 150-year-old farmhouse in Maine, a spiritual community in Oregon, an uptown apartment in Southern California, and for the past 23 years, a funky upstairs flat north of the Golden Gate Bridge, which she shares with her boat-rowing sweetheart. Along with painting & poetry Prartho has dabbled in such art forms as taxi driver, family therapist, Phys Ed instructor at Cornell University, housecleaner, single parent, head cook, amateur singer/song-writer, illustrator, and palm-reading psychic in various Catskill resorts.

Author of the award-winning collections *Indian Rope Trick*, *Elephant Raga*, and *Call from Paris*, and author/illustrator of the IPPY-winning gift book, *Causing a Stir: The Secret Lives & Loves of Kitchen Utensils*, Prartho's other published works include a poetry chapbook, *Garden Sutra*, a song/music/poetry CD, *Salt*, and a book of essays, *Everyday Miracles: An A to Z Guide to the Simple Wonders of Life*.

Poet Laureate Emerita of Marin County, California (2015-17), Prartho was awarded a 2005 Radio Disney Super Teacher award for her 22 years as a Poet in the Schools, the Marin Poetry Center's inaugural Rilke Award (2023) for nurturing the poets, a Marin Arts Council Individual Artist Grant in Poetry (2003), and an MFA in Creative Writing from Syracuse University (2013). She is founder of the ongoing poetry writing series: *The Poetic Pilgrimage: Poem-Making as Spiritual Practice*, now online. **www.prarthosereno.com**

The most dependable remark on Prartho's early report cards was "Easily distracted and distracts others"—a comment she has done her best to live up to.

Printed in the USA
CPSIA information can be obtained
at www.ICGtesting.com
JSHW081546171123
52183JS00001B/102

9 781421 835471